TAPESTRY LOOM TECHNIQUES

D1684952

In the broadest sense, weaving is simply the interlacing of fibers to
process can be done with the fingers alone, with a needle or on a loom with or without related
tools. Loom weaving implies, specifically, the interlacing of WARP, or stretched threads, and
WEFT, or filling threads. Loom weaving can further be divided into two categories:

MULTI-HARNESS or pattern weaving also referred to as LOOM CONTROLLED WEAVES:
Worked on looms having anywhere from two to sixteen or more harnesses through which
select warp threads are passed. A specific sequence of raising and lowering these harnesses,
individually or in groups, and then passing a filling material between each change, produces
the pattern. A repeated sequence or cycle of these shed changes determines the final
design. There are many pattern books which describe these patterns in terms of threading
and treadeling (changing of harnesses). Patterns can be designed in terms of texture,
color or both.

TWO-HARNESS or graphic weaving commonly referred to as WEAVER CONTROLLED
WEAVES: This approach can be considered as "free spirit" weaving. While the warp threads
remain taut and fixed at both ends, the weft threads are free to wander through these warps
in a myriad of ways for the sole purpose of expressing the images of feelings dictated by
the weaver. The results can be as severe as any pattern weave or can be a free expression
of joy. The finished piece can be, specifically, tapestries, wall hangings, bags, belts, rugs,
garments or virtually any fabric based article. The techniques involved are not definitive
but rather innovative, with expression the prime consideration.

It is the latter category that this book is primarily involved with. The TAPESTRY LOOM is
basically a two harness loom and thus is the basic tool for this expression. Tapestry loom
weaving has the potential of being the most creative of weaving techniques requiring maximum
involvement of the weaver. While many of these weaver controlled weaves are worked using
alternating sheds, many weaves are controlled by the fingers alone. The hands must thus
become directly involved with the fibers of the fabric. An intimacy between the weaver and his
work is the rewarding result of this pursuit. The therapeutic value in terms of creativity and
self expression should be welcome by both the young and the old. This creativity can find its
expression in terms of design or in the exploration of materials, color, textures and stitches,
or a comfortable combination of all these elements. The techniques described are meant only
as a guide to areas for exploration by the weaver.

THE TAPESTRY LOOM

While the tapestry loom is a two harness or shed loom, not all two harness looms are suitable
as tapestry looms. This book shall not go into the setting up of any particular loom, as the
manufacturer's directions should give this detail as specifically related to their loom. In
considering any loom for graphic weaving the following aspects are of the utmost importance:

TENSION: The warp threads must be held in a uniform and taut tension. As weft threads
are passed and become involved with these threads, there will be a tendency for them
to be deformed from their straight path and thus will either stretch or shorten. This is
commonly known as take up and will vary with the specific stitches used as well as with
the type of thread used. Provision must be made to control this tension as the weaving
progresses. Without such provision, weaving is limited to short lengths or damage to the
loom and/or threads is likely. Something has to give.

FIBER CAPABILITY: Warp threads in much weaving are selected primarily for strength.
In graphic weaving, selection is also based on color, texture and weight. These threads can
be completely hidden or primarily exposed. Selection can range from fine threads to heavy
cords. The mechanics of the loom should not limit your selection of materials.

WARP SPACING: With such a variety possible in warp selection, spacing of the warp threads
should be absolutely flexible. Aside from the warp material selected, spacing can vary
solely on the basis of the particular weave or stitches. Warp faced weaves can require 40
or more threads per inch while tapestry weaves work best with 4 or 5 threads per inch
using the same material.

SHED: If a shed changing device is incorporated into the loom, consideration should be given to the size of the opening (distance between lifted and normal threads at the heddles). If the shed is not large enough there can be confusion in respect to the individual threads in regards to which side of the shed they should be on. This is particularly critical when working with a soft, fuzzy warp. Some looms require the use of a thin flat stick or 'shed stick' which is inserted in a small shed and then rotated 90° to form a larger opening. Although this mechanically works, it unnecessarily adds to the operation of the loom rather then expediting the flow of the weaving. Some weaves are best manipulated with a thin long shuttle, while other weaves involve primarily a finger manipulation. A good open shed, about 1-1/2" will take much of the effort out of these manipulations.

SIZE: The physical dimensions of the loom will always limit the width of the weaving. Length, however, need not be limited by the mechanics of the loom. Any loom should be capable of handling virtually any length of warp. Long warps are generally rolled up or bundled as required during the weaving process. In considering width limitations, a loom with less then an 18" weaving capacity will prove to be frustrating. Narrower work can always be produced on a wider loom.

EXPOSED WARP: Graphic type weaving, while sometimes worked directly over a drawing or cartoon, is most often improvised or worked from a non-scale sketch or drawing. This latter approach requires a large portion of the warp to be exposed as the work progresses to assure continuity of the design. On many multi-harness looms, geared primarily to repeat patterns, the working distance is generally very short with the work being rolled up soon after the weft is passed. These looms are not at all suited to graphic weaving. By the same considerations it is advantageous to have a flexible shed changing system, one which can move along the frame in reference to the weaving edge. This capability will permit use of the maximum area of the loom frame opening.

WARPING: Because of the simple two shed arrangement required for graphic weaving, it is advantageous to be able to prepare your warp directly on the loom. As the warp is generally prepared from a single ball or skein of yarn, the set-up proceedure should allow for the passage of the yarn ball in a continuous fashion. Harness assemblies requiring the threading of this yarn through 'eyes' or slits will prevent the use of the continuous warp and will require the tying of each individual warp thread.

TOOLS

Graphic or design weaving can be worked without any tools and it is sometimes a good discipline to work in this fashion. To keep your weft yarn in order, it can be wound into a simple compact BUTTERFLY as shown and passed through the open shed from hand to hand. Since there is always an easier (or at least different) way to do anything, and as there have been and are many weavers, various tools or accessories have come about to ease the weaving process. Some of these tools will have general use while others might be used to work only one stitch. Any device whether found or improvised or purchased, which aids in the weaving process should be considered a weaving tool. As weaving becomes more a part of you and you the weaving, these tools will automatically accumulate. Some specific types of tools which should be considered are:

COMB: The weft threads can be pushed into place with a finger, but a comb will save much time as a wider area of the work can be manipulated at once. A good comb should have smooth dull teeth spaced wide enough apart so as not to bind on the weft threads. For a dense weave, a heavy comb is desirable as it will also serve as a beater to pack the threads in place. An ordinary table fork is often substituted for the comb.

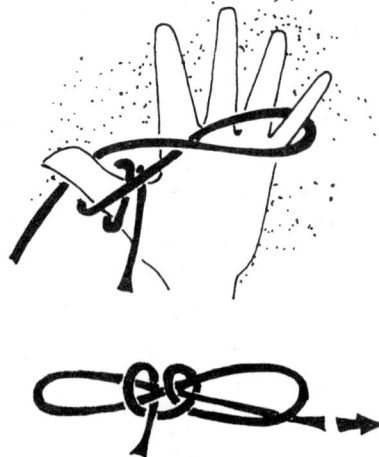

THE BUTTERFLY

BEATER: In warp faced weaves, the warp threads are packed too tight for the use of a comb. In this type of weave, a beater, which is generally a knife edged piece of wood, is used to open the shed to beat the weft in place. With end notches of some sort, the beater can also double as a shuttle. In Navajo weaving, an elongated comb is referred to as a beater. The long length permits a swinging action to beat the weft in place.

WINDERS: The winder is the simplest form of shuttle and much easier to use then the wound butterfly. The wound winder is a tight firm bundle easy to pass through the shed. These are inexpensive and can even be improvised from pieces of stiff cardboard. They work well for many of the finger manipulated weaves and are ideal when many different colors are worked.

 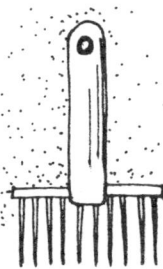  

COMB   COMB/BEATER   TAPESTRY WINDER

SHUTTLE: The shuttle is the basic tool for storing and passing the yarn and can be found in many forms. In tapestry loom weaving shuttles are generally limited to the following:

ROUND TAPESTRY SHUTTLE, also referred to as a needle or netting shuttle: This type of shuttle is probably the most useful for tapestry loom weaving. It not only stores the yarn but also serves as a needle for picking up select threads in specific stitch patterns.

FLAT STICK SHUTTLE: This is the most common type of shuttle and is best suited for simple weavings where the weft is passed from selvege to selvege. It holds the most yarn and, if the width of the weaving, will permit the passing of the weft across all warp threads in a single pass.

FLAT TAPESTRY SHUTTLE: Similar to the stick shuttle, this type has one end pointed and a side opening for the winding of the weft. This is specifically designed for the working on a vertical loom since the shuttle will not unwind when left suspended from the work. In looms with small sheds, this shuttle eases the passage of the weft. The flat tapestry shuttle will hold less yarn than a comparable flat stick shuttle.

BOBBIN: In addition to serving the shuttle function, the bobbin, with its pointed end, also serves as a beater. A narrow shaft stores the weft while the pointed end serves as a

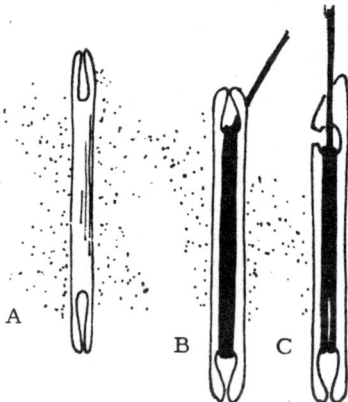 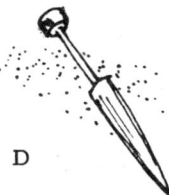 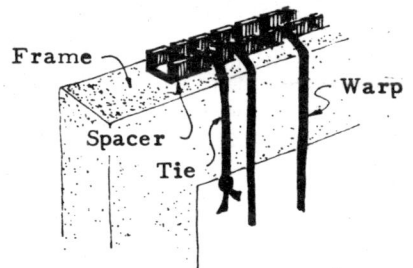

SHUTTLES
A. Round Tapestry
B. Flat Stick
C. Flat Tapestry
D. Bobbin

SPACER

needle for passing the thread and for pushing it into place. With the weft hitched at the neck of the bobbin, this type of shuttle will not unwind when left suspended from the work. Used primarily in high warp tapestries, these bobbins are ofter referred to as Gobelin bobbins after the French high warp tapestry studio.

Since the weft and shuttle become a single working unit, a shuttle, winder or bobbin of some type is required for each different color or type of thread used.

NEEDLES: The needle doesn't store the yarn but is used to pass the weft through tight areas, specifically near the end of the work, where the shed is minimum and in some of the more intricate stitches. The needle is also useful for joinings and for corrective work in the finished piece. The weaving needle characteristically has a large eye (for the heavy yarns) and a dull point. A sharp pointed needle is easily dulled on some sandpaper or concrete. Some common needle types are:

BENT TIP, also referred to as a Navajo or sacking needle: Particularly suited for working when no shed is formed. The curved tip facilitates the picking up of select threads.

STRAIGHT NEEDLE: A wide variety of straight needles are available. They are available in flat or round form. in wood or steel and in a wide range of lengths. These needles are best suited when working in an open shed and when a long needle is required.

LENO NEEDLE: This needle is specifically designed for the working of the lace weaves. It has a hook on one end and an eye on the other. The hook is used to pick up a warp for twisting over another warp while remaining within the shed.

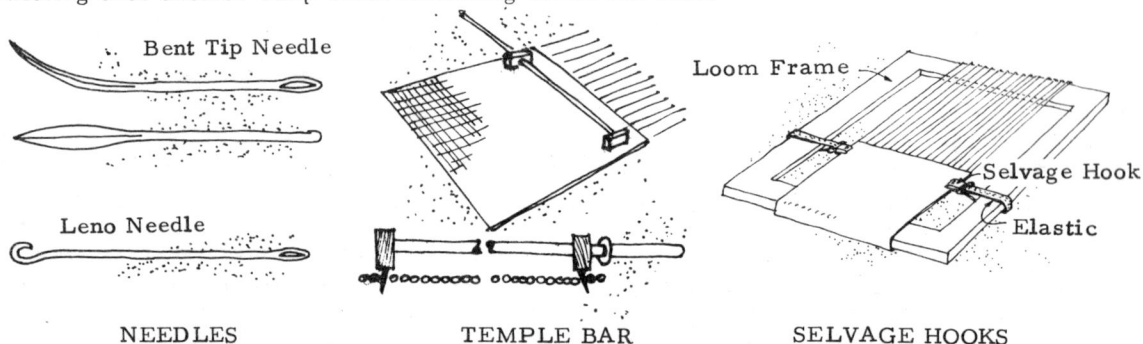

Bent Tip Needle

Leno Needle

NEEDLES

Loom Frame

Selvage Hook

Elastic

TEMPLE BAR

SELVAGE HOOKS

SPACER: A device to uniformly space warp threads and keep them from tangling when the warp is prepared directly on a frame. Nails, a stretched spring or notches in the edge of the frame are often used. A Nylon Spacer Strip is a precision device specifically for this purpose. It is easily attached. requiring no hardware, maintains an accurate spacing and will not cause damage to any surfaces to which it might come in contact. A spacer can be used on one or both wrapped edges.

TEMPLE OR STRETCHER BAR: Control of the selvege takes a great deal of skill. When the weft is passed and pushed into place it is formed into a wave pattern as it goes over and under the warp threads. This shortens it and, if proper allowance is not made, it will pull in the edges of the work. Until control is mastered. the edges can be periodically tied to the sides of the loom in a lacing fashion or they can be held in alignment by a temple bar. The bar has hooks which grab into the edges of the work and then keeps these edges spread by some locking device. The bar is easily placed and removed and is moved up and kept near the working weft as the work progresses. While most have width limitations, the KLIOT temple bar can be adapted to virtually any weaving width.

SELVAGE HOOKS: An alternate device used to maintain control of the weaving edge. The advantage over the temple bar is that there is no obstruction of the work, an important consideration in tapestry weaving. The selvage hooks, which require a rigid loom frame, are secured to the side members with adjustable elastic bands and attached to the woven edge by a spring clip.

PICK-UP STICK: This is a pointed stick, generally flat and narrow but sometimes round, used to work through complex warp manipulation such as in the lace weaves. A straight weaving needle of leno needle is often used for this operation.

SHED STICK: In primitive looms and in looms having a small shed, a thin flat stick is used to open and maintain a large shed. This shed stick is inserted flat and then turned on edge to spread the warp threads.

LOOM TYPES: There are three basic forms of the tapestry loom:

TABLE LOOM: Generally requiring the use of a table or stand as a support, the loom is worked at an essentially horizontal or inclined position. Some looms have the capability of being handled as lap looms while sitting on the ground. The table loom is generally the least expensive type and tends to be light weight and portable. Shed changing is always performed with the hands. The shed changing device can be simply groups of looped strings through which select warp threads pass, or individual rods to which these loops or HEDDLES are secured and which, in turn, are lifted up and down and held in either position by some supporting device. The lateral opening between the raised and lowered threads is the SHED through which the WEFT is passed. Most of the shed changing systems for table looms are cumbersome and awkward to manipulate, requiring several operations. More effort and time is generally relegated to the mechanics of the loom then to the creative aspect of weaving. The unique table loom which overcomes these mechanical drawbacks is the KLIOT Tapestry Table Loom which incorporates a patented shed changing device which automatically changes the position of warp threads to either of two sheds or a no shed position with a single operation

FLOOR LOOM: This is an essentially horizontal loom with its own supporting legs. The shed changing is worked by foot manipulation via foot peddles. The obvious advantage of this loom is that the hands need never leave the working area thus permitting maximum continuity of the work. The best looms of this type have the shed changing system entirely below the work leaving the working level free of any obstruction. The patented KLIOT Floor Loom incorporates these features and in addition, has the ability to fold flat for transit or storage with or without the weaving in place. Another advantage of this particular loom is that the work can be removed and resecured to the loom at any time. This can be an important consideration if more than one person is to use the loom or if more then one project is being worked on.

VERTICAL LOOM: The vertical loom can range from the Navajo type where the weaver sits squatted on the floor, or the high warp type on which the largest tapestries are executed. Traditionally, looms of this type use only a single heddle rod which supports the heddles for the alternate shed, the main shed being automatically formed by a figure '8' wrapping of the warp. This rod is spaced out a short distance from the work and is supported from the two side members of the loom. The alternate shed is formed in small sections by pulling, by hand, select groups of heddles.

MATERIALS

There is no definition or limit in regard to what materials can be used for graphic expression. The warp must have the ability to withstand the working tension but that is the only limitation. A smooth warp is easier to handle then a fuzzy warp but a fuzzy warp should not be discounted if it is necessary as a design element. If the warp is to be completely concealed, as in the tapestry weaves, there is no reason not to use a smooth cord of cotton, linen or similar material. Any yarns of at least 2-ply, nylon monofilament, braided cords, or even fine wire can be considered as a warp material.

The weft, except in warp faced weaves (discussed later), can be of virtually any material. Materials need not even be limited to fibers. Twigs, sticks, bones, feathers, leaves, grasses, unspun cotton, aluminum can pull tabs, beads...all can be used as weft elements in the execution of a design.

WEAVING TECHNIQUES

The WARP (stretched threads) should be as taut as possible without causing damage to the threads or loom. A tight warp produces a clear shed even with fuzzy yarns and facilitates the beating into place of the weft warns. When the weft is passed through these stretched threads it is distorted in an undulating fashion which casuse it to shorten. Allowance must be made for this shortening so as to prevent the edges of the weaving from pulling in. If there is too much allowance, a loose sloppy selvege will result. The correct handling of the weft takes a great deal of skill and will take time to perfect. A good technique for passing the weft is to lay it in the shed in a curved or arched fashion as shown, holding on to the selvege end while pulling the free end. Without closing or changing the shed, beat or push the weft into place starting at the center of the curve and working toward each end. The size of the arch will depend on the yarn you are using, the spacing of the warp and the particular weave technique. Try various arch shapes till control is achieved. Until your technique is perfected, you can maintain parallel edges by periodically lacing the edges to the side frame members or by using a temple bar.

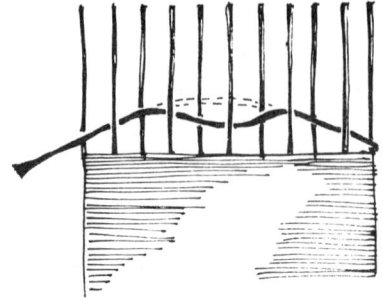

WEAVES

As applicaple to tapestry loom weaves, two gereral classifications of weaves can be considered: OPEN SHED or loom controlled weaves which involve the passing of the weft through alternate sheds, and CLOSED SHED or finger weaves which involve intricate manipulations of the weft around singular or groups of warp threads. These are general categories as there will be some overlapping where some of the finger weaves are worked in alternate sheds.

OPEN SHED WEAVES: In this category three techniques can be considered:

TABBY WEAVE: Sometimes referred to as a 50:50 weave, it is the simplest of the loom controlled weaves. The warp and weft threads are equally exposed in the finished piece. Warp and weft spacing is generally the same and thus a medium density warp of 8 to 12 threads per inch (using a medium weight yarn) is generally used. After each pass, the weft is pushed into place but not beaten. This is the most common weave worked on multi-harness looms designed for pattern weaving. A variation of the plain tabby weave is the TWILL weave. The simple twill, which is easily worked on a 4-harness loom, can be worked on the tapestry loom using a weaving needle to pass the weft in a closed shed position. The twill weave has a characteristic diagonal pattern.

TABBY WEAVE

TWILL WEAVE

WARP FACED WEAVE: This is a dense weave where only the stretched warp threads are exposed in the finished weave. A dense warp of 20 to 30 threads per inch (using a medium weight yarn) is generally used. This type of weave is also referred to as an inkle weave, although the inkle weave specifically refers to narrow bands. In the warp faced weave, the warp undulates while the weft is pulled taut after each pass. This causes a good deal of take-up or shortening of the warp and tension has to be adjusted accordingly. Rather then a comb, the weft is beaten into place using a knife edge beater in the open shed. A variation of this type of weave is card weaving. In this method groups of warp threads are twisted

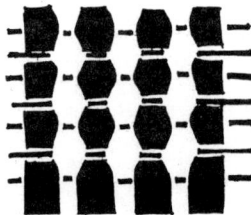

WARP FACED WEAVE

around each other or twined between each pass of the warp. Because of the extensive take-up in the warp faced weave and particularly the card weave, it is a common backstrap loom technique.

WEFT FACED WEAVE: As implied, the weft faced weave exposes only the weft with the warp being completely covered by the heavy beaten weft. A wide spaced warp of from 4 to 8 threads per inch (using a medium weight yarn) is generally used. This is the most common weave on the tapestry loom and is generally referred to as a tapestry weave.

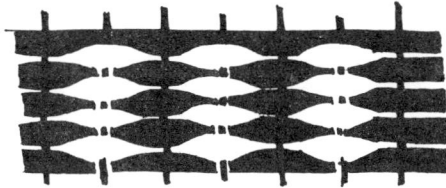

WEFT FACED WEAVE

Although all of the above techniques can be worked on the tapestry loom, the weft faced will be found to be the most useful for graphic designs. In setting up your loom, warp spacing should be set accordingly.

CLOSED SHED WEAVES: The weaves in this category can be classified as follows:

LOCKING WEAVES: The warp threads are held in a fixed relation to each other by the weft.

WRAPPED WEAVES: The weft passes over or under the same warp thread two or more times.

PILE WEAVES: The weft projects in a loose form above the surface of the work.

LACE WEAVES: The weft is used to open the warp to create an open-type fabric.

KNOTTED WEAVES: This is essentially the use of macrame techniques based on the half-knot and square knot. The stretched warp threads serve as the holding cords around which the knots are formed.

The above classifications should not be considered as absolute but only as a reference for organization and exploration. The examples illustrated are in no way meant to be definitive but rather a guide for further exploration by the weaver. There are areas of overlapping and areas yet to be explored. The prime objective should be to convey the idea of the weaver. The justification of any technique is that it serves to satisfy this idea.

For purposes of clarity, most weaves and stitches are illustrated in a open or loose form. They are not intended to illustrate the finished appearance of the weave but rather to illustrate how it is worked. Although some of the weaves can be left loose as a casual design element in the work, most require beating into place for security.

TAPESTRY WEAVES

The tapestry weave is the classic weave for depicting represantational or abstract designs. It is a loom controlled weave as alternate sheds are formed through which the weft thread is passed. Color and texture comes primarily from the types of weft yarns used. Each change in color or texture requires a corresponding change in weft thread. The techniques of the tapestry weave are thus primarily concerned with this point of change.

Technically and traditionally a true tapestry weave is identical on both sides. Any technique not having this symmetry could not be considered a tapestry weave. The back of the tapestry, however, is always considered as the top face of the weaving. All cut ends of the various weft threads are left extending on this surface.

Although the tapestry weft thread is always beat into place to completely cover the warp, an open or tabby weave is shown in the following diagrams for clarity.

VERTICAL CHANGES: Several techniques can be considered, each having its own characteristics in terms of line detail and ease of working.

SLIT: This is the simplest technique for color change. Adjacent color threads return on the last boundry warp thread of their color area. The slits can be left open, with the openings forming part of the design, or they can be stitched on the surface (back of the piece) with a fine thread. The advantage of this technique is that each color area can be woven independently using a single shuttle. The SLIT gives the straightest line at a color change. The slit is commonly referred to as a Kelim or Kelim technique.

INTERLOCKED WEFT: The weft threads of adjacent areas are alternately crossed between two adjacent warp threads before they reverse direction. Weaving of adjacent areas must be done simultaneously, adjacent color threads working in the same direction.

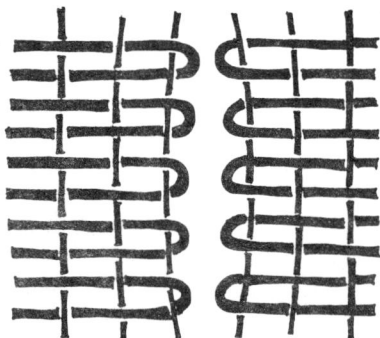

SLIT   INTERLOCKED WEFT

LOCKED WEFT: Adjacent contrasting weft threads are crossed in the same sequence between two adjacent warp threads before they reverse their direction. Adjacent wefts are carried alternately towards and away from each other with a lock made at each meeting. The underside (front) will have a clean vertical line while the upper or working face will have a double line.

DOVETAIL: Adjacent weft threads alternately wrap around a common warp thread before they reverse their direction. This joins adjacent sections and produces a fine toothed pattern at the juncture. Because of the extra thread on this common warp, there will be a slight ridge at the juncture. The weaving of both adjacent areas must proceed together.

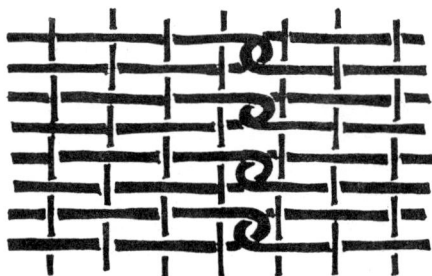

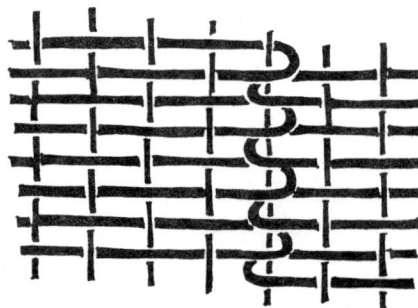

LOCKED WEFT   DOVETAIL

MULTIPLE DOVETAIL: Similar to the dovetail but with groups of threads from each color area alternating the wrapping. This creates a large toothed juncture while at the same time reducing the boundry ridge. The obvious advantage is that several rows can be woven with one weft thread before working on the adjacent area.

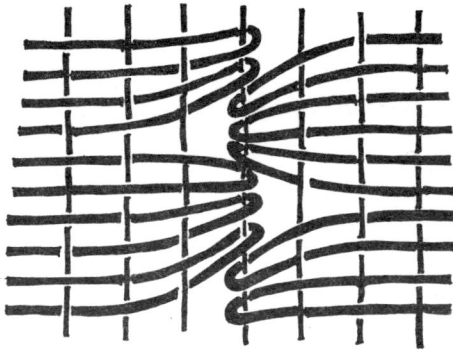

MULTIPLE DOVETAIL

DIAGONAL CHANGES: No locks are required as the movement of the boundry line across the warp threads automatically seals the joining. If narrowing areas are worked first, it is possible to work entire single-color areas at a time. The slope of the diagonal will depend on how many warp threads each row advances. For steep diagonals, slits will be formed as the advance will not occur at every row.

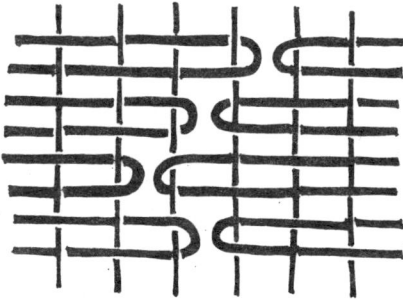

DIAGONAL CHANGE

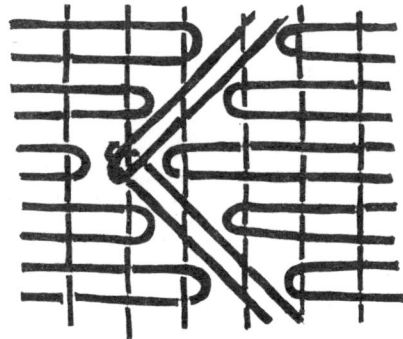

DIAGONAL OUTLINE

DIAGONAL AND VERTICAL OUTLINE: Two continuous weft passes are made along the boundry. Care must be taken in placing these threads to prevent puckering.

   LIMNING: An outlining technique where the weft is wrapped around the warp thread. This is necessary for steep diagonals and vertical lines.

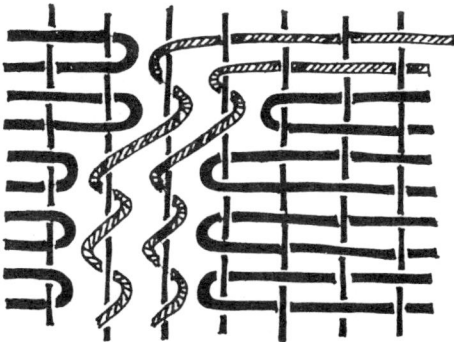

LIMNING

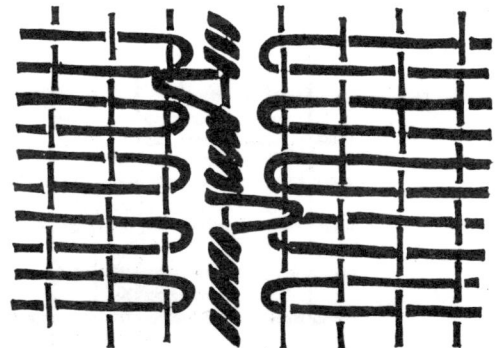

INTERLOCKING WEFT
WITH LIMNING

INTERLOCKING WEFT WITH LIMNING: For a vertical line a single warp thread is tightly wrapped and periodically interlocked with an adjacent warp.

SPOTS AND LOZENGES: Small spots can be formed by weaving the background continuously and then crowding the contrasting spot thread. For larger spots, the background is modified by curved diagonals so as to prevent puckering.

SPOTS

WEDGE WEAVES: This is a useful technique when the oblique weaving line is a conceptual part of the design. Clean diagonal lines are produced by this technique. Care must be taken to keep distortion to a minimum.

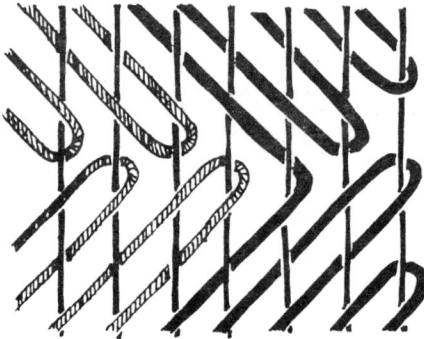

WEDGE WEAVE

BROCADE: This is a laying-in technique where an additional weft thread of contrasting color or texture is worked along with the normal weft within a designated pattern area. This technique is generally used on a plain or one color background. The laid in thread weaves back and forth through the specific design area while the normal or background weft weaves from selvege to selvege.

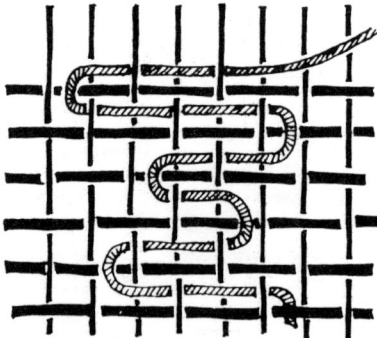

BROCADE

PAIRED WEFTS: Common in Coptic tapestries for tweed effects, two contrasting color weft threads are worked together. With their relation to each other controlled, many distinct patterns can be made. If they are run straight with corresponding colors of adjacent rows the same (the pair is twisted at the end of the row), horizontal lines will result. If corresponding colors of adjacent passes alternate, spots will be formed. Pattern changes within a row is easily controlled by select twisting of the paired threads.

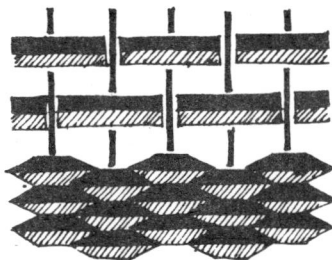

HORIZONTAL LINES   SPOTTED   PATTERN CHANGE

LOCKING WEAVES

The two general categories of locking weaves are Chaining and Twining, as worked with the weft threads. They are termed locking because they lock the warp threads in relation to each other. In addition to forming specific design patterns, either of these weaves can be used at the ends of the warp to serve as warp spacers. Chaining is similar to crocheting, where a series of loops is formed which, in turn, are interlocked with each other. In twining, weft threads, in groups of two or more, twist around each other and the warp threads as they cross them.

CHAINING: Three basic variations of chaining can be considered.

   BASIC CHAIN: In its simplist form, this chain is worked with a single color weft in a closed shed, with each chain loop being formed around one or more warp threads. The starting end of the chaining thread is anchored to the warp by weaving or knotting across one or more warps. The leading end is then drawn under the remainder of the warps. Holding the free end, pull up loops between select warp threads, pulling each, in turn, through the previous loop. Two or more wefts of contrasting colors can similarly be used to form the chain, where each successive loop, or other sequence, is formed by a different color thread in alternating fashion.

BASIC CHAIN

   SURFACE CHAIN: This chain is commonly formed around alternate warps, leaving the intermediate warp uninvolved. It is thus best worked in an open shed. The following row is then worked around the raised warps of the alternate shed. Twill effects can be achieved in this manner. This chain can also be formed around other warp patterns, such as every warp, every third warp, etc. Compared to the basic chain, this technique results in a greater relief as it appears to lie on the surface of the work.

SURFACE CHAIN

WARP ALIGNED CHAIN: Loops are pulled up in alternate rows of weft, which are, in turn, interlocked into the loop of the previous row. The chain sequence is terminated by interlocking it with a normal weft pass. The loops can be interlocked without a prior twist or they can be twisted before interlocking. There are many variations of this technique, with many possibilities for surface patterns. If weft loops are pulled up in each row, the loops will stagger producing diagonal lines in the work. Pairs of loops can be joined and interlocked with a common loop to produce many complex lacy designs. The use of contrasting color wefts should also be considered where color can be controlled by pulling up select color weft threads from the background. Another extension of this technique is to form large loops which can then be twisted to form a cord which in turn can travel on the surface of the work before being interlocked.

WARP ALIGNED CHAIN

TWINING: Twining is worked without sheds, two or more wefts twisting together before and after crossing on both sides of the warp threads. Depending on which direction the threads are twisted, the angular direction of the pattern can be controlled. Specific design effects can also be achieved by using contrasting color threads. The contrasting colors can be made to arrange themselves in adjacent rows in various spot or angular patterns (see also PAIRED WEFTS under Tapestry Weaves). This control is achieved by the number of twists the paired wefts are given at the selvege before they return into the work and by the direction of the twist as the wefts cross the warps. Reversing the twist while crossing a row will produce diamond designs.

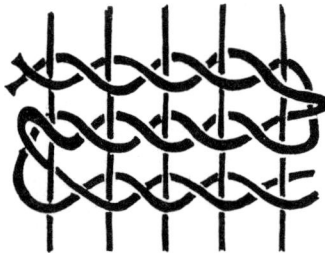

TWINING

TANIKO TWINING: This is a distinct variation of the twining technique. Two contrasting colors are normally used, one wrapping around the other which, in turn, is pulled taut so it remains straight. The wrapped color will be the primary surface color. To change the surface color, the two colors are given a half-twist and the alternate color does the wrapping. In a similar manner, three or more colors can be controlled to produce more intricate patterns. It should be noted that the wrapping color weft only wraps around the back or straight weft, never around the warp.

TANIKO TWINING

WRAPPED WEAVES

Wrapping techniques are used to give a raised surface on the work and a contrasting or diagonal direction to the weave. Characteristic of most of these stitches is the difference in texture on the two sides of the weaving. Used as a rug weave, the wrapped stitch provides a good dense wearing surface. Many of the pile weaves are the direct result of cutting the surface loops as formed by the wrapped weaves. The wrapped weave is often referred to as the Soumak. It is strictly weaver manipulated and worked with the warp in a no-shed or neutral position.

ORIENTAL SOUMAK: This is a basic wrapping of one or more threads and can be worked in either direction. Consecutive rows can be wrapped or the Soumak can alternate with rows of plain weave for strength. The working side is generally considered the finished side. The packed stitches have a sloped appearance resembling a twill. The direction of slope is determined by the method of wrapping as well as by the direction in which your are working. The number of warp threads enclosed within each loop will determine the angle of slope of the stitch . The stitch illustrated is worked by going over two warps and then under one and is referred to as a 2/1 Soumak. Other common patterns are the 4/2 Soumak and the 6/2 Soumak.

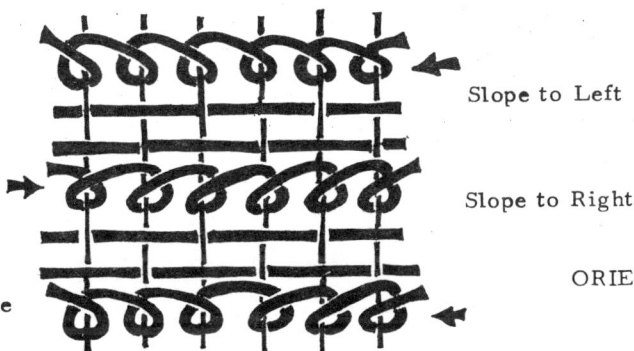

Slope to Left

Slope to Right

ORIENTAL SOUMAK

Change of Slope

EGYPTIAN SOUMAK: This is essentially the reverse of the Oriental Soumak as it leaves the rib effect on the surface of the work, with the heavy ridge on the back.

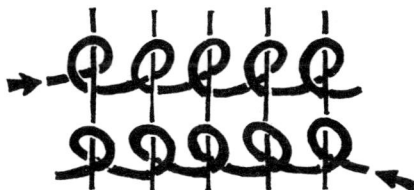

EGYPTIAN SOUMAK

DOUBLE LOCKING SOUMAK: The weft wraps around more than one warp thread and produces a heavier ridge in the design.

DOUBLE NON-LOCKING SOUMAK: Resulting in a softer ridge, this wrapping is similar to the wedge weaves (see TAPESTRY WEAVES).

DOUBLE LOCKING SOUMAK

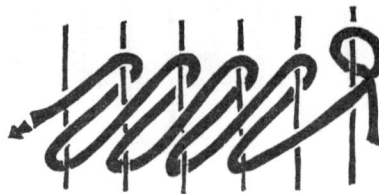

DOUBLE NON-LOCKING SOUMAK

SINGLE SOUMAK (SWEDISH KNOT): Generally worked on the back side, the effect is a twill pattern somewhat less pronounced then in the Oriental Soumak as the wrapping tends to pack down to a near horizontal position.

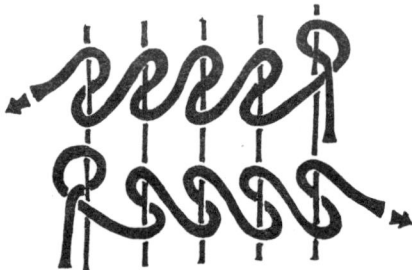

SINGLE SOUMAK

BUSHONGO SOUMAK: This variation is a combination of the Oriental and Egyptian Soumak. The effect is a thin angular ridge on the surface of the work.

BUSHONGO SOUMAK

GREEK SOUMAK: This is a vertical wrapping with two or more knots or wraps made on the same warp before proceeding to the next one. Although the most common pattern is three wrappings on each warp, variations can be made in terms of number of wraps and number of warps included in each wrap. This technique tends to open the fabric while providing a heavy dense surface which is stiff enough for use in rugs.

GREEK SOUMAK

PILE WEAVES

Simulating the fleece or hair of an animal, the pile weaves are used where long wearing qualities are required as well as where the soft shag appearance is desired. In addition to the obvious use of pile weaves in rugs, these weaves can be effective for garments either in whole or as trim. By the nature of the techniques involved, pile weaves can be simply extending loops or strands (where the loops are cut). Pile weaves are generally combined with a foundation or plain weave which forms the structure of the fabric. This plain weave is generally concealed by the fullness of the extending pile.

PULLED UP LOOPS: This is the simplest pile technique as the passed weft weft is simply pulled up between select warps before the shed is changed. In pulling loops in a row, always start at the previous selvege, as much weft will be drawn into the work as the loops are formed. For uniformity, the loops can be pulled over a gauge such as a flat stick, dowel or crochet hook. This is removed after the completion of the next plain row, If your loop is long enough, and your yarn has a medium to hard twist, these loops will tend to twist on themselves. If the loops are arranged in a vertical or near vertical pattern, they can be chained together as discussed under LOCKING WEAVES.

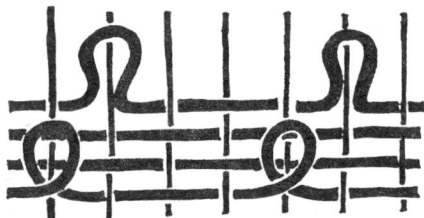

PULLED UP LOOPS

GHIORDES KNOT: This is the most common of the knotted piles and is used to make RYA rugs, where rows of cut pile alternate with rows of plain or tapestry weave. The two basic methods of forming this knot on a stretched warp depend on whether the yarn is pre-cut or continuous. With pre-cut yarn, each length is cut approximately 1/2" more then twice the pile depth and then wrapped over select warp threads. This is a preferable method when many colors are worked across a row. When continuous yarn is used, the loops are generally formed around a pile guide (although the fingers can be used alone) and then either left as a looped pile or cut to form a cut or shag pile. By the nature of the knot, the pile will tend to fall in one directon or another depending on how the knot is tied. Since color is more intense when looking into the end of cut yarn, the work will have different appearances when viewed from opposite directions. This knot can also be tied sideways by forming it around a single warp. Worked in other textile forms, this knot can be formed with a needle in a solid canvas backing or by a "latch hook" in an open mesh canvas.

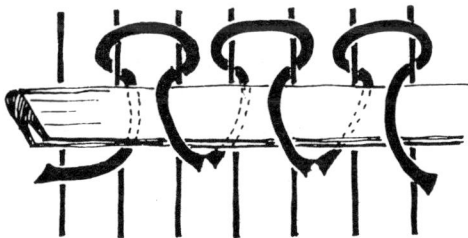

From Continuous Yarn

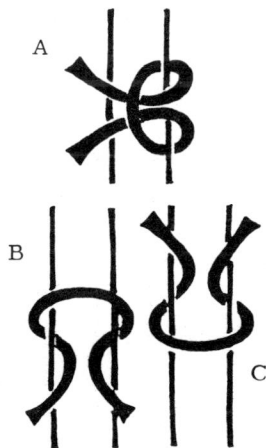

A. Sideways Knot
B. Down Knot
C. Up Knot

GHIORDES KNOT

Density of the work can be controlled in several ways. In addition to pile length and weight of yarn, density can be controlled by the spacing of the knots. Formed around skipped warps, density will be decreased . The most common variation is to form it around every other warp thread. This is easily done by working the knot with the shed in the open position. If alternated with a plain weave, the knots will lay over this weave eliminating a gap at the edge (see EDGES). The densest pile is formed when adjacent knots wrap around a common warp.

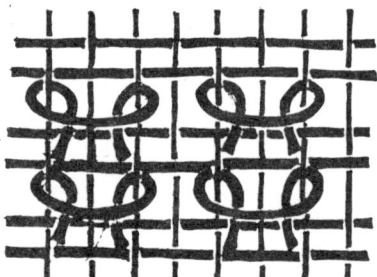

Formed in Open Shed

Dense Pile

GHIORDES KNOT

SEHNA (PERSIAN) KNOT: Although not as common as the Giordes, this knot produces a more even texture to the work. As with the Giordes, it can be formed from pre-cut or continuous yarn. The Sehna pile, by its nature will fall in a angular direction in reference to the warp.

From Continuous Yarn

SEHNA KNOT

SPANISH (SINGLE WARP) KNOT: This simple knot and its variations is formed around a single warp thread and is generally worked in an open shed position using alternate warps. In the following row, the alternate warps which were not used in the preceding row, would be used. Rows of plain weave are necessary between rows of knots to keep them in place. The staggered pattern of knots gives the fabric a generally uniform appearance.

FRENCH KNOT: A variation of the single warp knot which is somewhat more secure.

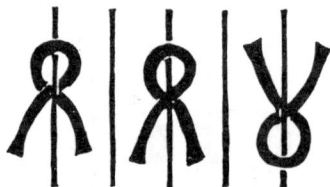

SPANISH KNOT

FRENCH KNOT

CUT SOUMAK: This knot, formed by cutting the Oriental Soumak wrapping, is similar to the Ghiordes but with each end falling in an opposite direction. This knot thus eliminates the directional aspect of the Ghiordes knot.

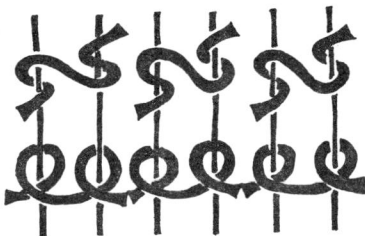

CUT SOUMAK

LAID-IN PILE: Although not a knotted pile, and the least secure of all pile techniques, this simple method is useful when heavy and/or bulky materials such as lengths of roving or strips of cloth are used to form the pile. A firm plain weave is necessary between rows to keep the pile material in place.

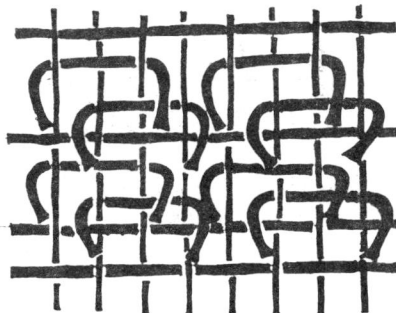

SCOTTISH PILE: This is a specific laid-in pile technique where the pile material is laid in open sheds under two warps. Each third row is a plain weave.

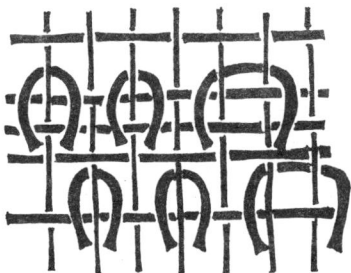

LAID-IN PILE   SCOTTISH PILE

LACE WEAVES

The lace techniques are used to form open type fabrics or open areas to contrast with dense woven areas. As these techniques involve manipulation of the warp threads, which are left exposed, selection of the warp material must be considered in terms of the design.

LENO (GAUZE) WEAVE: This is the simplest and most common of the lace weaves. Two adjacent warps are twisted and then the weft is passed to keep the twist in place. The direction of the twist alternates in each row in order to prevent the warp from building up a twist at

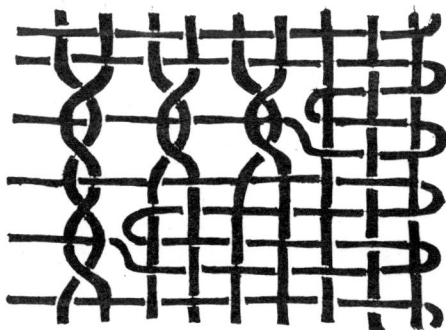

LENO WEAVE

the far end. In one row the back warp is picked up first and the top warp dropped. In the following row, the top warp is dropped and then the back warp is picked up. Thus the warps do not twist around each other but rather simply cross. A weaving needle, a pick-up stick or better yet, a leno needle will simplify the picking up of the desired warp threads. Variations of this weave involve the twisting of groups of warp threads resulting in a more open design. The leno weave can be worked from selvege to selvege or only in specific areas. In the latter case, additional rows of plain weave are used to fill in the spaces around the open areas. Since there is considerable take-up in the twisted warps, some attempt should be made to even out the leno woven areas across all warps. If this is not possible an adjustment of the non-twisted warps will be required to maintain uniform warp tension.

TARASCAN (MEXICAN) WEAVE: This is a more elaborate form of the leno weave as it involves the twisting of non-adjacent pairs of warp threads. In its simplist form one thread from each side of the shed is crossed in succession with one or more threads between each twisted pair. This is accomplished by starting alternate rows with an initial crossing formed with one thread from one shed and two or more threads from the other shed. All other crossings or twists are with one thread from each shed. Twists are worked as in the leno weave.

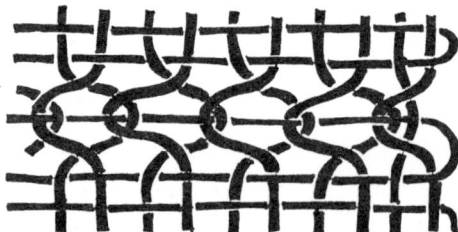

TARASCAN WEAVE

DOUBLE TARASCAN WEAVE: This is a more elaborate form of the Mexican weave where pairs of threads are crossed in alternate rows and single threads crossed in the inbetween rows.

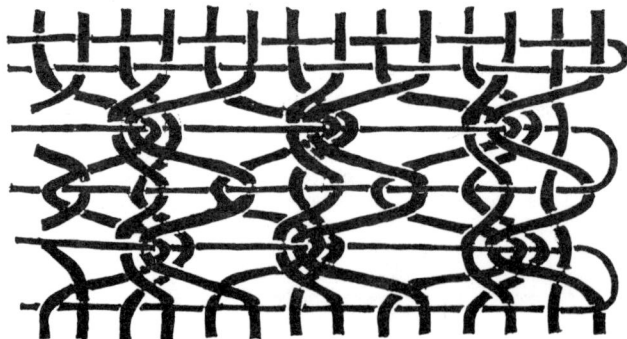

DOUBLE TARASCAN WEAVE

SPRANG: Sprang is not truely a weave since weft threads are not required. If the Tarascan twisting techniques are worked by twisting the warps always in the same direction, the warps will interlock and maintain their relation to each other without the use of a weft. Twisting in this manner will produce a corresponding but mirrored twist at the far end of the warp. After the twists for one area are completed, a few rows of plain weave or chaining is required to keep the warps from untwisting. The resulting fabric has a tendency to collapse but can be held in an open position by surrounding woven areas. This is a useful technique for working open warp areas at the completion of a weaving where straight wefts would be distracting. (reference: SPRANG, LANGUAGE AND TECHNIQUES, Kliot. Some Place).

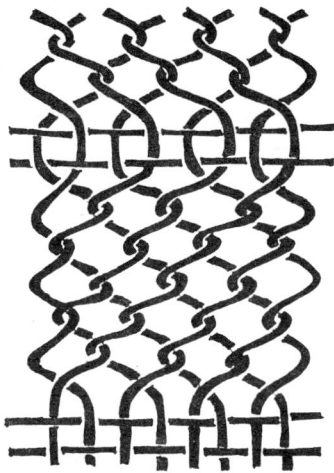

SPRANG

SPANISH LACE: This is a dense lace form more akin to weaving. Blocks are woven in a tight fashion forming wide slits between adjacent areas. Adjacent rows of blocks can be aligned or formed from half the warps from each of the two adjacent blocks in the preceding row.

Aligned Rows

SPANISH LACE

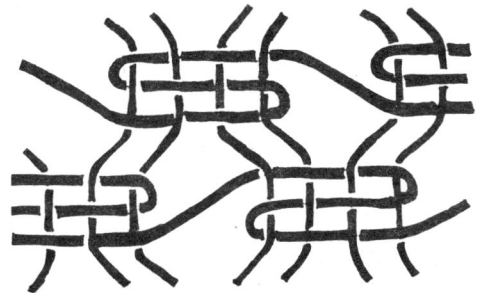

Staggered Rows

WARP TIES: Areas of exposed warp can be tied into groups to form open patterns. These can be tied independently or, if adjacent, by a common warp or tie cord. The tieing can be done as the work progresses or at the completion of the work. In large hangings with open areas, this simple technique will prevent woven areas from slipping on the warp.

WARP TIES

KNOTTED WEAVES

Many of the techniques of macrame can be used on the tapestry loom to create strong vertical lines as well as open lacy patterns. The weft threads will run vertically, knotting around a single or group of warp threads. These groups can be redivided in successive rows to create an open weave.

HALF KNOT: This is the basic knot and is formed by an under-over motion of the weft around the warp. It can be worked as a right over left motion or a left over right motion.

HALF KNOT   SQUARE KNOT SENNIT   HALF KNOT SENNIT

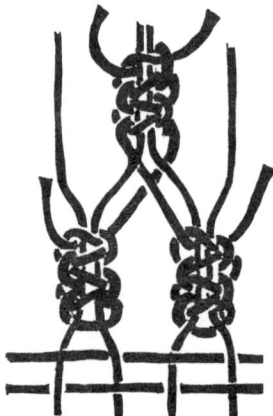

SQUARE KNOT SENNIT: This is a heavy flat band formed by working, alternately, right and left half knots in succession around a common group of warps.

HALF KNOT SENNIT: This is a spiral band formed by working right or left half knots in succession around a common group of warps. The type of half knot worked will determine the direction of the spiral.

BEADS

It is often desirable to incorporate beads into the work. For optimum control these are best incorporated with the weft. The beads can be held in place by any of the several methods shown. The bead weft can be wrapped around the warps; bead rows can be supported by adjacent rows of plain weave; double weft threads can be used to encircle each warp; the bead weft can be held in place by the twisting of warps; or beads can be separated by multiple warps.

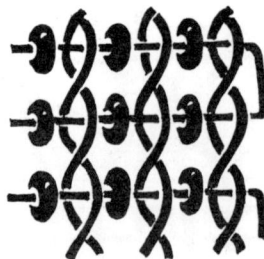

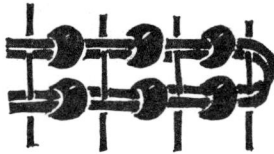

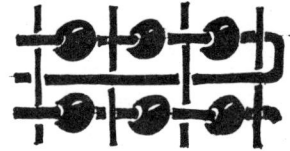

EDGES

Although the edge or selvege can be left with no additional treatment, there are instances where special consideration to this detail should or must be made. For large pieces, and specifically rugs, it is a good practice to use double threads for the last two warps. This minimizes distortion and stretch of the finished work.

ARGATCH: In knotted weaves and lace weaves there will be voids at the selveges if these weaves are carried completely across the row. These voids, called the argatch, need to be filled to add strength and weight to the piece. Many methods are possible with consideration being given to decoration as well as function. There are two basic approaches, one uses the same thread as the plain weave while the other uses a separate thread. In the latter method a more decorative and/or heavier thread can be utilized.

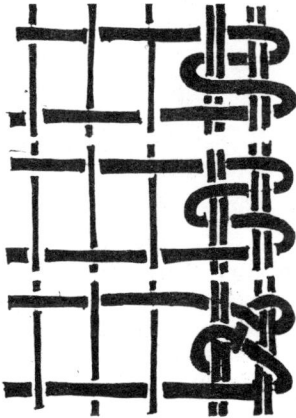

From Same Thread

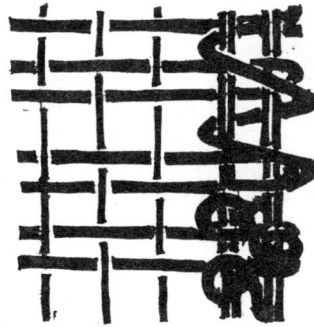

From Separate Thread

ARGATCH

JOININGS

All looms will place a limit on the weaving width as determined by the physical size of the frame. For wider pieces, lengths of narrower woven pieces are joined together. This joining can be purely functional and made inconspicuous or it can be an important decorative element in the finished piece. A weaving needle is commonly used for these joinings.

BLIND JOININGS: The techniques illustrated show the common methods for making an invisible joining. Using a matching thread, the stitch is pulled tight enough so the adjacent pieces will come together without overlapping. This is commonly used when joining sections of pile weaving where the joinings are covered by the pile.

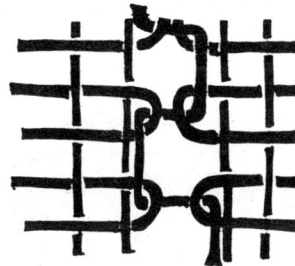

BLIND JOININGS

DECORATIVE JOININGS: In joining many of the flat weaves, it is virtually impossible to make the junction completely invisible. It is a more realistic approach to design the joining as a motif. Decorative stitches as well as contrasting color threads can be used in such instances. In the design of panchos and other items of clothing, widths of the woven panels should be considered in relation to the finished garment.

LACING: A simple lacing, using contrasting color or weight of thread, can form a decorative juncture. For a more elaborate detail with a raised rib, this can be combined with a knot to form a knotted lacing. The points of attachment can be parallel to the juncture or they can undulate to further enhance this detail.

COUCHING: This is essentially a binding or wrapping of the seam. The seam is covered entirely with a resultant raised rib. The joining can be worked with a simple whip stitch or a more elaborate stitch such as a buttonhole, chain or cross stitch.

STITCHERY: Many of the common stitcherey stitches can be used to join sections of the work or to overlay a blind joining.

PLAIN LACING   KNOTTED LACING   COUCHING

ENDINGS

Aside from any decorative effect, two considerations must be made in terminating the free warp ends. The weft must be secured so it will not loosen or unravel; and the extending warps must be protected from unraveling and wear. Where wear is not a concern, the latter consideration can be relegated to decorative effect.

OVERHAND KNOT: This is a quick simple termination which adequately secures the weft. Groups of warp strands are knotted as close as possible to the end weft. It is a good plactice to have adjacent threads of each group cross to further secure this weft. The groups can be of uniform size or arranged in some studied pattern.

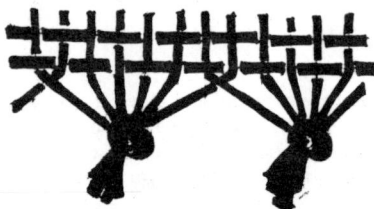

OVERHAND KNOT

PHILIPPINE EDGE: This is a series of continuous knots extending from one selvege to the other, each knot being formed over the previous two extending warps. Although one row is sufficient to hold the warps, additional rows can be formed to create a wider band. If always worked from the same side, this band will shift on a diagonal. If the work is turned over, and always worked from the same side each time the work is turned, this shift can be avoided. This edge results in a raised ridge on the working side.

PHILIPPINE EDGE

HALF DAMASCUS EDGE: Starting at one selvege and working to the other, each warp is wrapped around the adjacent warp so it is turned back on itself. These ends can then be bound or darned to prevent unraveling. The result is a smooth edge without an extending fringe.

DAMASCUS EDGE: If the Half Damascus is repeated, the ends will again return, this time in a direction away from the weaving. These ends can then be fringed. This is a handsome edge with a ridge formed on both sides of the piece with the warp ends emerging between them. For a wider edge, the Damascus can be repeated.

HALF DAMASCUS EDGE

DAMASCUS EDGE

INDIAN EDGE: This is similar to the Half Damascus with the exception that the returned end is brought out leaving extending warps pointing away from the work.

INDIAN EDGE

SEWING: Where warp ends are too short to knot, a tight sewing can be made using a needle and a separate thread. The stitch wraps around each warp and is then pulled close to the edge of the piece.

SEWING

WOVEN AND DARNED EDGE: For a neat edge without any raised border or fringe, each warp can, in turn, be woven over the adjacent several warps and then darned back into the fabric.

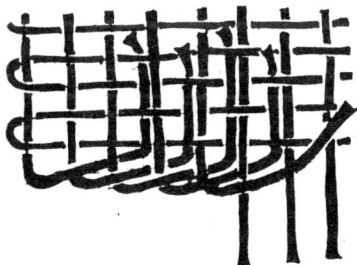

WOVEN AND DARNED EDGE

FRINGE: Groups of extending warps can be protected by combining them in various ways. Some of the more common techniques are:

OVERHAND KNOT: The overhand knot can be repeated to form simple or complex interlaced patterns.

LASHED OR WHIPPED FRINGE: Groups of threads can be tied together by a wrapping technique using the same or a contrasting thread.

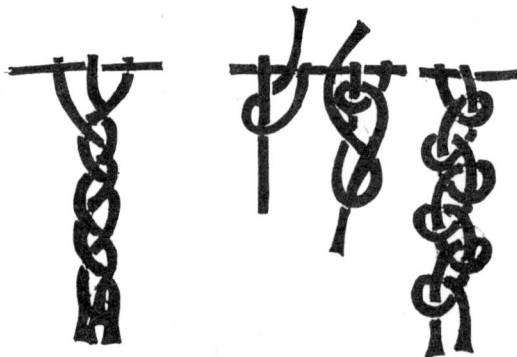

BRAIDED FRINGE: Threads can be braided and, if necessary, finished off with a short end-wrapping, half hitches or an overhand knot. The three thread braid is the most common with each thread of the braid consisting of two or more warps.

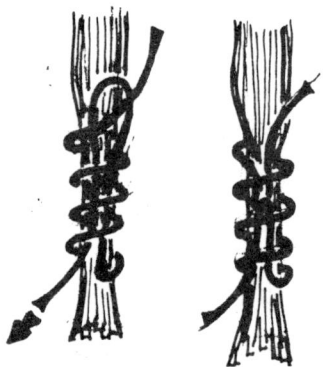

LASHED FRINGE   BRAIDED FRINGE   KNOTTED FRINGE

KNOTTED FRINGE: Again three groups of warps are worked. Alternate hitches are worked to create a knotted decorative fringe having a bulky appearance. This fringe takes up a great deal of warp so it can only be worked with extra long warp ends.

WEAVING TERMS

DARNING: Weaving an extending thread into the finished work using a needle.

HARNESS: A support for the heddles which, in turn, support select warp threads. Raising or lowering the harness will raise or lower the select threads.

HEDDLE: A tie through which an individual warp thread is passed and which is used to raise or lower this warp thread. Can be manipulated by hand or through a harness.

PLAIN WEAVE: A simple under-over weave worked with two sheds. It can be either a tabby or tapestry weave depending on the particular piece. It is generally referred to as a plain weave when used as a background for a design or as a filler between decorative weaves.

SELVEGE: The edge of a weaving lying parallel to the warp.

SETT: The warp spacing referring to the number of warp threads per inch.

SHED: A lateral opening in the warp formed by the raising and/or lowering of select warp threads.

WARP: The stretched lengthwise threads. These are the structural or supporting threads of the weave.

WEFT (WOOF): The crosswise threads which weave across the warp. Also referred to as the' filling thread.